Praise for *One Minute Mentoring*

"If I could go back and tell the twenty-year-old version of me one thing it would be 'Get a mentor.' I think it's one of the most important things you can do and I'm so glad Claire and Ken are shining light on the process."

—Jon Acuff, *New York Times* bestselling author of *Do Over: Make Today the First Day of Your New Career*

"Life's journey doesn't need to be a lonely walk. Being a mentor is your opportunity to share your learning moments to help someone step into the best version of their personal self, and it feels good doing it! *One Minute Mentoring* lays out your path to becoming an effective mentor."

—Garry Ridge, CEO of WD-40 Company and co-author of *Helping People Win at Work*

"Ken and Claire have given us a fresh take on mentoring in their inspiring new book, *One Minute Mentoring*—and I am grateful."

—Francis Hesselbein, President and CEO of the Frances Hesselbein Leadership Institute and former CEO for the Girl Scouts of America

ONE MINUTE MENTORING

Also by Ken Blanchard

THE NEW ONE MINUTE MANAGER
with Spencer Johnson, MD, 2015

COLLABORATION BEGINS WITH YOU
with Jane Ripley and Eunice Parisi-Carew, 2015

LEGENDARY SERVICE
with Kathy Cuff and Vicki Halsey, 2014

FIT AT LAST
with Tim Kearin, 2014

TRUST WORKS!
with Cynthia Olmstead and Martha Lawrence, 2013

GREAT LEADERS GROW
with Mark Miller, 2012

LEAD WITH LUV
with Colleen Barrett, 2011

WHO KILLED CHANGE?
with John Britt, Judd Hoekstra, and Pat Zigarmi, 2009

HELPING PEOPLE WIN AT WORK
with Garry Ridge, 2009

THE ONE MINUTE ENTREPRENEUR
with Don Hutson and Ethan Willis, 2008

THE 4TH SECRET OF THE ONE MINUTE MANAGER
with Margret McBride, 2008

LEAD LIKE JESUS
with Phil Hodges, 2007

LEADING AT A HIGHER LEVEL
with the Founding Partners and Consulting Partners of The Ken Blanchard Companies, 2007

KNOW CAN DO
with Paul Meyer and Dick Ruhe, 2007

SELF LEADERSHIP AND THE ONE MINUTE MANAGER
with Susan Fowler and Laurence Hawkins, 2005

ONE SOLITARY LIFE
2005

THE SECRET
with Mark Miller, 2004

CUSTOMER MANIA!
with David Novak and Jim Ballard, 2004

THE ON-TIME, ON-TARGET MANAGER
with Steve Gottry, 2004

THE LEADERSHIP PILL
with Mark Muchnick, 2003

FULL STEAM AHEAD!
with Jesse Stoner, 2003

THE SERVANT LEADER
with Phil Hodges, 2003

ZAP THE GAPS!
with Dana Robinson and Jim Robinson, 2002

WHALE DONE!
with Thad Lacinak, Chuck Tompkins, and Jim Ballard, 2004

THE GENEROSITY FACTOR
with Truett Cathy, 2002

HIGH FIVE!
with Sheldon Bowles, Donald Carew, and Eunice Parisi-Carew, 2001

MANAGEMENT OF ORGANIZATIONAL BEHAVIOR
with Paul Hersey, 8th edition, 2000

BIG BUCKS!
with Sheldon Bowles, 2000

THE ONE MINUTE MANAGER BALANCES WORK AND LIFE
with Dee Edington and Marjorie Blanchard, 1999

THE 3 KEYS TO EMPOWERMENT
with John Carlos and Alan Randolph, 1999

LEADERSHIP BY THE BOOK
with Bill Hybels and Phil Hodges, 1999

THE HEART OF A LEADER
1999

GUNG HO!
with *Sheldon Bowles, 1998*

MISSION POSSIBLE
with *Terry Waghorn, 1996*

EMPOWERMENT TAKES MORE THAN A MINUTE
with *John Carlos and Alan Randolph, 1996*

EVERYONE'S A COACH
with *Don Shula, 1995*

RAVING FANS!
with *Sheldon Bowles, 1993*

THE ONE MINUTE MANAGER BUILDS HIGH PERFORMING TEAMS
with *Don Carew and Eunice Parisi-Carew, 1990*

THE ONE MINUTE MANAGER MEETS THE MONKEY
with *William Oncken, Jr., and Hal Burrows, 1989*

THE POWER OF ETHICAL MANAGEMENT
with *Norman Vincent Peale, 1988*

LEADERSHIP AND THE ONE MINUTE MANAGER
with *Patricia Zigarmi and Drea Zigarmi, 1985*

PUTTING THE ONE MINUTE MANAGER TO WORK
with *Robert Lorber, 1984*

THE ONE MINUTE MANAGER
with *Spencer Johnson, MD, 1982*

Also by Claire Diaz-Ortiz

DESIGN YOUR DAY
2016

THE BETTER LIFE
2015

HOPE RUNS
2014

TWITTER FOR GOOD
2011

KEN BLANCHARD
AND CLAIRE DIAZ-ORTIZ

ONE
MINUTE
MENTORING

HOW TO FIND AND WORK WITH A MENTOR
- AND WHY YOU'LL BENEFIT FROM BEING ONE

Thorsons

Thorsons
An imprint of HarperCollins*Publishers*
1 London Bridge Street
London SE1 9GF

www.harpercollins.co.uk

First published in the US by William Morrow,
an imprint of HarperCollins*Publishers* 2017
This edition published by Thorsons 2017

10 9 8 7 6 5 4 3 2 1

A catalogue record of this book is available from the British Library

ISBN 978-0-00-814681-8

Printed and bound in Great Britain by Clays Ltd, St Ives plc

MIX
Paper from
responsible sources
FSC **FSC® C007454**
www.fsc.org

FSC™ is a non-profit international organisation established to promote
the responsible management of the world's forests. Products carrying the
FSC label are independently certified to assure consumers that they come
from forests that are managed to meet the social, economic and
ecological needs of present and future generations,
and other controlled sources.

Find out more about HarperCollins and the environment at
www.harpercollins.co.uk/green

CONTENTS

A NOTE TO READERS   11

INTRODUCTION   13

PART I

NO COMPASS, NO MAP: LIFE IN A
   MENTORLESS LAND   19

ASKING FOR DIRECTION   24

WHO ME, A MENTOR?   30

THE SEARCH   39

THE FIRST MEETING   46

MISSION IMPERATIVE   54

ENGAGEMENT: ESTABLISHING THE RELATIONSHIP   61

TAKING TIME FOR INTROSPECTION   71

SPEAKING YOUR TRUTH   77

LEARNING TO NETWORK   84

BUILDING TRUST   94

NETWORKING DONE RIGHT   100

SHARING OPPORTUNITIES   107

REVIEW AND RENEWAL   118

MENTORING NEVER ENDS   125

PART II

THE MENTOR MODEL   135

**CREATING A MENTORING PROGRAM IN
    YOUR ORGANIZATION**   142

COACHING VERSUS MENTORING   146

ACKNOWLEDGMENTS   149

ABOUT THE AUTHORS   153

SERVICES AVAILABLE   157

JOIN US ONLINE   159

A NOTE TO READERS

One Minute Mentoring is a fictional parable about the power of finding—or being—a mentor. Perhaps you're wondering about the title. Why *One Minute* Mentoring? Because we have found that the best advice we ever gave or received was given in less than a minute. In other words, the guidance that really made a difference did not come in the form of long, complex theories—it came in short, meaningful insights.

INTRODUCTION

Are you feeling less than certain about the path forward in your career? Are you wondering if you really have what it takes to reach your goals? Are you wondering what your goals should be? Then perhaps it's time you found a mentor.

Maybe you answered all the above questions with a resounding, "No!" If so, perhaps it's time you *became* a mentor.

The Business Hall of Fame is filled with the names of people who discovered that finding a mentor made all the difference in reaching success, as well as the names of leaders who attained greatness by mentoring others. You can be in that good company.

Most people agree that having a mentor is a good thing, but they don't know how to find one or use one.

And while most agree that *being* a mentor is a good thing, they don't think they have the time or skills to do so.

That's why we wrote this book: to give readers simple knowledge and easy-to-use tools to find and leverage mentoring relationships.

No matter what kind of mentoring you get involved in—new hire, peer-to-peer, adult-to-adolescent, or cross-generational—we know that it can positively transform not only your life, but the lives of others as well.

What is cross-generational mentoring? That's when a young person is paired with an older person, so they both can learn and grow. Ken is a leadership expert in his midseventies and Claire is a former Twitter executive in her midthirties, and that makes us a living example of the lessons we are teaching. Through our own mentoring partnership—and through others—we have personally experienced the life-changing power of this practice. That said, we do want to point out that the age spread doesn't have to be as wide as ours for mentors and mentees to get value out of the relationship.

In *One Minute Mentoring*, we tell the story of Josh Hartfield, a young sales rep whose motivation is flagging, and Diane Bertman, a sales executive whose crammed schedule isn't delivering the satisfaction it once did. As the story of Diane and Josh unfolds, readers will learn the six action steps to creating a successful mentoring relationship, as well as key insights such as:

- How to find a mentoring partnership—whether you are a mentee seeking a mentor or a mentor seeking a mentee.
- How to work with a mentoring partner to make the positive changes you want to see in your work and life.
- How to apply succinct, One Minute mentoring advice.
- How to tap into the wisdom and skills of people from all age groups and backgrounds.

Successful people do not reach their goals alone. Behind even the most independent achiever is a person or group of people who helped that person succeed. So no matter your age, we encourage you to start finding a mentor today.

We also encourage you to mentor someone else, because those who extend a helping hand to others have much to gain. In the words of an ancient Buddhist proverb, "If you light a lamp for someone, it will also brighten your own path."

If you are ready to build a powerful mentoring relationship and watch your work and life transform, then read on!

KEN BLANCHARD
coauthor of *The New One Minute Manager®*
CLAIRE DIAZ-ORTIZ
author of *Twitter for Good*

PART I

NO COMPASS, NO MAP: LIFE IN A MENTORLESS LAND

Josh Hartfield sat at his desk and stared at his computer screen, paralyzed about what to do next. His in-box contained fifty priority e-mails. He had seven urgent voice mails from existing clients, and he needed to finish a new presentation before a sales appointment on Friday.

In terms of work, he had plenty. In terms of motivation, he had none. It wasn't exactly the ideal frame of mind to be in for his quarterly review, which was coming up in five minutes.

"Ready?"

Josh looked up to see his boss, Eva Garcetti, who managed western regional sales for their company.

"Sure," Josh said with a halfhearted smile.

He followed Eva into her office and took a seat facing her imposing mahogany desk.

"Let's not beat around the bush, Josh. Your numbers this quarter have been mediocre at best. This is becoming a pattern with you. What's going on?"

"Just a slump. I'm pulling out of it," he said, doing his best to believe it.

Five years after joining JoySoft as a sales rep, Josh was treading water. His job was stale, and he was no longer progressing in his career.

"I've heard that before, Josh. I think you could use some help. I recommend you spend some time with Eric. He set a new sales record last week."

Josh tried not to wince. Eric Aguilar was the upstart new sales rep now sharing a cubicle with him. Eric was just a year out of college, and already he was outperforming Josh two to one. So Josh wasn't surprised by Eva's recommendation. Still, it was depressing to think that he was in such bad shape that he was being told to take pointers from a new hire.

—

Do some personal reflection about what your strengths and weaknesses are.

—

"I know my suggestion might sound discouraging, but I'm concerned about you, Josh. It's like you've lost your motivation. The first few years you were doing all right. As you know, though, sales isn't for everybody as a long-term career."

Josh swallowed hard.

"What are you getting at, Eva? Should I be dusting off my résumé?"

"Not necessarily. What I'm suggesting is that you do some personal reflection about what your strengths and weaknesses are. By spending more time with Eric, you can get a sense of why he's doing so well."

"Beginner's luck?" Josh said with a weak grin.

"I don't think so. Seriously, why don't we talk again after you've had some time to think about how you can either get your numbers up or maybe redirect your career energies? I'd like to help in either case."

Walking back to his cubicle, Josh reflected on Eva's advice. He hadn't always felt so discouraged. Back when he had just graduated from college with a degree in business, he'd had all the energy in the world. The results of a vocational preference test indicated that he might be good in sales, which led him to a job as a junior sales rep at JoySoft. He'd fantasized about becoming a top salesperson.

Five years later, reality was staring him hard in the face. At this point, he was just hoping he could hold on to his job for another year or two—enough time to figure out what he *really* wanted to do.

As Josh entered his cubicle, Eric was pumping his fist in the air.

"Signed!" Eric shouted happily, slamming down the phone. He pulled out a red marker and drew a big X across the day's date on his wall calendar. As Josh had learned from Eric, the calendar was a motivational tool he'd picked up from a business book. Every X represented a new client. According to Eric, the more Xs in a row you got, the more likely you were to get more.

Eric had a lot of Xs this month.

Good thing I don't have one of those calendars up, Josh thought.

With a sigh, he picked up his mug and headed for the break room. He needed a breather from Eric's enthusiasm. As Josh refilled his mug, he realized he was at a crossroads. He needed consoling—and good advice.

Fortunately, at times like these he knew just the right number to call.

ONE MINUTE INSIGHTS

Pause, Reflect, and Learn

- Where are you in your life? Are you on an upward trajectory, or have you hit a plateau?
- Do you feel uncertain about the direction you're heading?
- Are you open to learning from others?

ASKING FOR DIRECTION

"Dad, hi. It's me."

"Josh! Nice to hear from you. What's up?"

"I'm thinking about coming home for the weekend."

"Great! Your mom will be thrilled. And your brother's going to be here, too. What's the occasion?"

"Just want to get out of the city and see you guys. Maybe run a few things by you."

"Okay. We look forward to seeing you."

As Josh said good-bye to his father and pocketed his phone, he felt some of the tension he'd been carrying slip away. Not all sons had good parents. He was grateful to be one of the lucky ones.

*

A few days later Josh was gathered with his mom, dad, and older brother, Brian, around the barbecue.

"Josh, you said you wanted to run some things by us," said his dad as he flipped burgers. "What's cooking—besides what's on the grill?"

"I'm having some issues at work," Josh said. "These days, it takes all my effort just to get from nine to five. Eric—who shares a cubicle with me—is young, but he's getting better results than I am. I used to feel confident in my sales ability. Now, not so much."

His father looked up from his grilling. "Is there anything we can do?"

His dad had been a successful media executive for many years, and his mom was a middle-school principal. Josh respected their opinions more and more as the years went by.

"You're already helping, just by listening."

"Tell us more," said his mom.

"On bad days, I feel like I should throw in the towel. Those are the days when I wonder what I really do, anyway. What is my job, when you break it down? Just an endless series of e-mails and meetings and presentations? Does any of my work really matter?"

His parents said nothing, but he could tell by their thoughtful faces that he had their full attention.

"The thing is," Josh continued, "I'm just not sure what I should be doing with my life. How do I get out of this rut and get my career going again?"

—

When you have a problem to solve, talking about it is a good first step.

—

His mom said, "When you have a problem to solve, talking about it is a good first step. Maybe JoySoft isn't a good fit for you. Perhaps you just need a change of scenery. Have you thought about getting your résumé out there? Don't forget, you had a couple of good offers before you went with JoySoft."

"Yeah, I've thought about that. But what if the problem isn't the company, Mom? What if the problem is me?"

Josh looked over at his brother, who was helping himself to some barbecued chicken. "What do you think, Brian?"

"Sounds like you're having a classic late-twenties crisis. What helped me was working on my MBA. It gave me time to think about what I wanted to do. Plus, I made a lot of good job contacts. That's how I ended up in commercial real estate."

Josh said, "I don't think an MBA is in the cards for me right now. But I sure could use some good professional contacts. My boss wants me to take some pointers from Eric, my hotshot cubicle mate. His sales have been on fire since he started. You can imagine how that makes me feel—being told to take advice from someone who's five years younger than me."

"I know it might be tough on your ego, but actually, learning from Eric would be a good interim step," said his dad. "For the long term, though, it would be ideal to find an older mentor who could give you some big-picture advice about your career and life. Think of how much you've helped Ricky."

Two summers ago Josh had become a "Big Brother" to twelve-year-old Ricky through the Big Brothers Big Sisters program.

"But Ricky's just a kid," said Josh. "I need grown-up help."

"I've been saying that for years," his brother kidded. "But Dad's right—you need a career mentor. When I was hired, my company immediately set me up with a mentor who had the job they wanted me to grow into, because they needed as many knowledgeable brokers as they could get. I'm learning so much faster than I could have on my own."

"All right," said Josh. "I'll find a mentor. But where?"

"Maybe your boss can refer you to one of the company's older, successful salespeople," said his mom.

"Or you could ask your roommate for some contacts," said his dad. "He's a big networker."

"But Dev is in engineering," Josh objected.

—

Potential mentors are all around you once you start looking for them.

—

"You never know where a good mentor might come from," said his dad. "My first mentor was one of my high school teachers."

"Mine was a businesswoman who lived next door," said his mom. "People who can help you see the big picture don't necessarily have to be in your field."

"That's right," said his dad. "Potential mentors are all around you once you start looking for them."

ONE MINUTE INSIGHTS

Pause, Reflect, and Learn

- Would a mentor help take you to the next level?
- Setting an intention to get help is an important first step in the mentoring process.
- A mentor doesn't necessarily have to be in your chosen field.
- As you search for a mentor, make sure you turn over every stone. Think about former supervisors, college alumni, teachers, professors, neighbors, friends, family, company programs, professional associations, volunteer organizations, and online mentoring organizations.

WHO ME, A MENTOR?

Diane's plane touched down at LAX. It had been a whirl-wind trip—London, Amsterdam, Zurich, Chicago, and all the airports in between. Extensive travel was a way of life for a vice president of sales. As the flight attendant made announcements, Diane pulled out her phone, took it off airplane mode, and called her assistant.

Jocelyn picked up on the first ring and asked, "How'd it go?"

"Right now I'm exhausted, but I had some good moments. I was able to bring my best negotiation skills to the table to close that network deal."

"I knew you would," said Jocelyn.

"So what's my schedule for the rest of the week?"

"No travel, so that's good. But it is a busy one, I must say. Can you pull up your calendar? I just updated it."

Diane opened her calendar and scanned quickly for white space. Seeing none, she sighed.

After thirty-five years in sales, she relied on a competent executive assistant like Jocelyn to organize, prioritize, and "cut the fat," as she liked to say.

"Am I essential for that meeting on Thursday?" Diane asked. "I see Travis is on the attendance list. Can he handle it and report back?"

There was a pause on the other end of the phone. "Well," Jocelyn replied, "he did say it would really be better if you were there to meet the clients."

Diane sighed again, knowing this familiar conversation like the back of her hand. As the top sales executive at Quest Media, she was used to hearing that she was needed everywhere. But was she?

"All right," Diane said, "I'll be there. Got any other great news for me?"

"We still have to talk about the party," Jocelyn said firmly. "You can't keep putting it off much longer. We're getting close to the big day. I'd like to make it special, but I'm going to need your input."

"Oh, *that*." Again, Diane sighed. "We can talk about that tomorrow. I'll be in by nine."

Diane ended the call, staring at her blank phone. *I'm not even excited by my own birthday party*, she thought. *What's happened to me?*

She switched to her photos and looked at the newest

pictures of the twins. Their big eyes stared back at her and she shook her head, still not believing that she was finally a grandmother. She couldn't wait until they were old enough to smile.

I should take off a day before the end of the month to see Sarah and the girls, she thought. Or wait, when did she have to go on her next trip for those client meetings? Could she get the flights changed to see the twins on the way home? Probably not; the schedule was tight as it was.

For the tenth time that day, she sighed.

Maybe I'm getting too old for this. Should I retire? she wondered.

Diane had no idea. But she knew who might.

＊

Warren Riggs.

Diane—now settled in the backseat of the airport shuttle—searched for the name as she scrolled through her phone contacts. Once she found it, she tapped the number and waited for the line to connect.

I hope he's not out on the water, she thought. *I need him on the top of his game, not catching another fish.*

Warren Riggs was Diane's first boss. And he changed Diane's life. From the beginning, he believed in her. Even when she was a rookie—a clueless yet driven twenty-something who knew she wanted to be in the media industry but had no idea where to start.

From her very first day on the job, Warren saw something in her that others didn't. And over time, he helped her realize her own strengths by teasing out her passions and putting her on the track to become a blossoming television sales executive. When she switched jobs—leaving Warren after six great years—he stuck by her, never failing to offer advice, support, and clear direction just when she needed it. Diane didn't know where she'd be now, if it hadn't been for Warren.

"Hello?"

"I'm glad I caught you, Warren. I thought you'd be out on your boat."

"I should be!" Warren said with a laugh. "But I've been working all morning. Remember my semi-retirement party a few years ago?"

How could she forget? At that party Diane had met a number of people whose careers Warren had shaped over the years. She wasn't the only one who had him on speed dial.

"Of course I remember," said Diane.

"Remember that absurdly long-winded banner they had?" Warren asked.

"You mean the sign that said, 'Semiretirement at 80 Is the New Retirement at 65'?"

"That's the one. So you caught me semiworking," he said with a chuckle. "To what do I owe the honor of your call?"

"Oh, Warren. Sometimes lately it all seems too much. I'm on the road all the time. My poor husband hasn't seen me in weeks, and I'm missing my new grandchildren. I'm wondering whether or not I ought to semi-retire, too."

"What's your thinking behind that?"

"A lot of people my age are thinking about retirement, not an endless cycle of logistical gymnastics. My assistant tries to keep my schedule sane, but it seems to get worse every year. Frankly, I'm feeling drained. Things have been so hectic at work. I just don't have my old passion for the job anymore."

"Go on," said Warren.

"I always said I'd never retire at sixty-five. But now that it's only a few years away, I'm not so sure. Maybe I just need something to reenergize me. Is feeling burned out a reason to throw in the towel?"

"What do you see yourself doing if you retire?"

"I definitely want to spend more time with Sarah and the twins."

"But *all* your time?" Warren asked.

"Not really, but I keep hearing my friends' voices ring in my ears."

"What do these voices say?"

"They keep saying, 'Haven't you worked hard enough, Diane?' Everyone seems to be convinced that I should let my career take a backseat for once. I particularly get that message every time I forward people another beautiful picture of the twins."

Warren paused before replying. "What I hear you saying is that right now you have a lack of passion in your career, you're feeling overwhelmed, and you have the nagging sense that maybe it's time to put this whole work world behind you once and for all and hang up the big retirement sign on your door."

"That's about it. What do you think?"

She expected support from Warren, but his reply immediately put her on the defensive.

"I think you need more balance in your life. Right now, you're giving too much of *you* to your business. You need to share yourself with people outside of work."

"But I already do!" she answered, a little too quickly and a lot too loudly. "I donate to charity, I volunteer on holidays at the food bank, and I do my best to be available to friends and family—"

"Maybe I didn't make it clear. You don't need more items on your to-do list. You need to share who you are with others. Have you ever thought about being a mentor?"

"Warren! I need energy and focus, not another distraction."

"Here's the thing," Warren said. "If you find someone you genuinely want to mentor, that relationship will give you the energy you need."

"But who would I mentor?"

"How about a young person in sales? That will remind you why you got into the work in the first place—and show you how far you've come. And mentoring a young person will help you focus on your own next steps."

"Where would I find this person?"

"Just keep your eyes and ears open. Once you set your intention to be a mentor, you'll be amazed at the people who show up."

—

Mentoring another person will help you focus on your own next steps.

—

"Now that I think of it, over the years people have approached me about helping them. I've always turned them down, because I was too busy. And I'm still worried that I won't have time to do this well."

"Don't worry. Many people avoid mentoring because they think it takes a lot of time. It doesn't have to. Some of the best advice I ever received came from tidbits during casual conversations with my mentors."

Mentoring? Me? Diane still wasn't so sure. But it wasn't the first time she hadn't agreed with Warren right away. Over the years, she'd learned to take a breath before responding to big ideas—especially from Warren.

"All right. It scares me, but I'll try it. As long as I can count on you to walk me through it."

—

Many people avoid mentoring because they think it takes a lot of time. It doesn't have to.

—

"That's the spirit," Warren said. "Okay, I've got another call, so I have to run. But I'll see you soon. Don't you have a birthday coming up?"

"Yeah, but I haven't had time to plan a party."

"Well, if you have a party and I'm invited, I'd better not see any retirement signs up anywhere. At least not until you try mentoring someone first."

"It wouldn't be a party without you, Warren. And it won't be a retirement party—yet. Thanks for the pep talk."

ONE MINUTE INSIGHTS

Pause, Reflect, and Learn

- Have you avoided becoming a mentor because you think it takes too much time?
- Being a mentor—while it does require regular communication—isn't a full-time job.
- Most people are energized by their mentoring relationships; you likely will be as well.
- By setting the intention to find a mentee, you'll become more open to potential mentoring partnerships all around you.

THE SEARCH

When Josh got home to his apartment that night, Dev was tinkering with a computer on the dining room table.

"Replacing the hard drive," Dev explained.

As Dev worked, Josh told him about the conversation he had with his parents and brother about finding a mentor.

"My boss suggested I ask Eric, the young guy who shares my cubicle, to be my mentor. I don't mind learning stuff from him, but I'd love to find an older person with more extensive experience as a mentor. Someone who could help me figure out if sales is even the right career for me. Any suggestions?"

Dev took a moment to think. "Most of my contacts are tech geeks our age, so I don't think they'd be much help. But I do have an uncle who's been in sales for years. He's quite successful. Want me to introduce you?"

"Sounds like a good start," said Josh.

*

Two days later Josh was sitting in a restaurant with Dev's uncle, Ron, a sharply dressed man in his fifties. Ron certainly looked to be the picture of success.

"Dev tells me you're trying to decide if sales is right for you. Let me be the first one to tell you—if you want to make money, stick with sales! It's the only job where the sky's the limit. The rest of these jobs, they give you a salary and then you've got to beg at the end of the year for a bonus. *Beg!* My salary is under my control. It just depends on how hard I want to work and the number of sales I want to make. Period."

"I was hoping that would be the case with me," said Josh, "but I'm finding it easier said than done."

Ron pointed a finger in Josh's face. "Tenacity is what you need! It doesn't always come easy, so you gotta stick with it and put in the hours. What's getting in the way of you putting all your time and energy into your job? Are you living and breathing sales?"

"Well, I do have a life outside of work. I spend time being a Big Brother to a kid named Ricky. I also like to stay in shape, so I go hiking or play basketball with Dev and our friends on the weekends. It's good to keep balance in my life, right?"

"Forget balance! You've got to remember: sales is where the action is. The company depends on you. Once you're making big money *then* you can get some balance in your life."

The conversation went downhill from there. Dev's uncle was all about sales, sales, and sales—and he had no qualms about it. Whatever Josh said, Ron discounted it. It quickly became clear to Josh that Dev's uncle, however successful, was not someone he wanted to spend much time with, let alone have as a mentor.

Over the next several weeks Josh discovered it wasn't that easy to find a mentor. He talked to several people who came recommended by friends, relatives, and coworkers. None of them were quite right. Mismatched values, personality, work experience, and scheduling all played a part.

Still, he remained hopeful.

The breakthrough came one day when he dropped by the Big Brothers Big Sisters headquarters to pick up tickets for a game he was taking Ricky to. One of the counselors passed him in the lobby and asked, "How's it going, Josh?"

Josh couldn't help but let it all out.

"With my Little Brother, great. With my job, not so much."

"What's up?"

"Let's just say I'm not thriving. In fact, I've been looking for a mentor. Someone who can help me get my
career to the next level."

"You should talk to Linda Partridge. She knows
everybody," the man said without missing a beat.

"Isn't she the chapter president of Big Brothers
Big Sisters? I don't want to bother her with my
problems."

The man smiled. "You obviously don't know Linda.
She lives to serve people. Come on, let's walk over and
see if she's in her office."

*

Moments later Josh was sitting in front of Linda's desk.

"How can I help you?" she asked.

"I need career direction. I'm in sales right now, but
I'm not sure that's where I should stay. I've been looking
for a mentor, but finding one is easier said than done."

"What have you learned during your search so far?"

"I've learned what I *don't* want in a mentor just as
much as what I do want. I want a person who isn't just
successful, but who also cares about family and friends.
I'd like someone who has qualities I value like honesty,
generosity, and humor."

Linda nodded. "It's not always easy, but finding someone who matches your values and personality type is important."

"That's for sure. I met with one prospective mentor who was super focused on work, to the exclusion of everything else. Another guy I met with had no sense of humor and was completely focused on himself. He wouldn't let me get a word in edgewise."

—

It's not always easy, but finding someone who matches your values and personality type is important.

—

"Sounds like you need someone who's an excellent listener and who has the ability to focus on others."

"Does anyone come to mind?"

"Not at the moment. Let me think about it, though. I'll bet I can come up with a good candidate or two."

*

Later that week at the grocery store, Linda ran into her old college friend Diane Bertman.

"What a treat it is to see you!" said Linda.

"I'm afraid my schedule is so busy these days that the only time I manage to cross paths with you is at the Big Brothers Big Sisters annual fund-raiser," said Diane, shaking her head.

"Don't worry, Diane. I'm just grateful that you and Mark have always been such generous supporters."

Diane told Linda about her indecision around retiring. "My trusted adviser, Warren, suggested that I back off some of my focus on business and find a young person to mentor."

"It's interesting you mention that," said Linda. "The other day I was talking to one of our Big Brothers about his need for a mentor to get out of the slump he's in. You two might be a perfect match. He's in sales and isn't sure that's where he should spend his career. And you've been in sales but aren't sure that's where you should spend the rest of your life."

"What kind of person is he?"

"He's terrific. He's one of the best Big Brothers we have. He has a wonderful, caring heart. The kids just love him."

"Sounds promising."

"Tell you what. Why don't I set up a lunch for you two, and you can go from there?"

"I'm up for it if he is," said Diane.

ONE MINUTE INSIGHTS

Pause, Reflect, and Learn

- There are many different types of mentoring partnerships: peer to peer, adult to adolescent, apprentice to master, cross-generational, and mentoring within a company are a few. What you look for in a mentor or mentee will depend on the type of mentoring relationship you're seeking.

- Think about the key qualities you're looking for in a mentor or mentee before you begin the search. What values and personality characteristics are important to you?

- Be courteous to prospective mentors. If the two of you don't click, promptly communicate your decision and thank them for their time.

- Prospective mentees, *be brave*. When you ask someone to mentor you, the worst that can happen is you break even. If the person says no, you didn't have a mentor before, anyway!

THE FIRST MEETING

It's hard to say who was more nervous to meet that Monday at the Bayside Grill—Diane, fidgeting with her purse as she waited near the maître d' stand, or Josh, wiping his palms on his pants as he opened the front door of the restaurant and scanned for a woman fitting Linda's description of Diane.

After Diane and Josh were seated, they talked briefly about their mutual friend Linda and the good things she'd told them about each other. Once the server took their orders, Diane got down to business.

"Years ago, my first boss taught me that there are two aspects of working with someone else—essence and form," she said. "*Essence* is all about sharing heart-to-heart and finding common values. *Form* is about structure—how we might work together. Whenever I jump to form before exploring essence, it never seems to work out. So let's declare this lunch an essence meeting where we find out about each other—what we value and what's in our hearts."

—

Essence is all about
sharing heart-to-heart and
finding common values.
Form is about structure.

—

"I'm glad you're bringing this up," said Josh. "So far in my search for a mentor nothing's worked out, because I haven't felt that heart-to-heart connection you're talking about."

"So let's find out about each other," said Diane. "Tell me a little more about who you are."

Josh didn't answer right away. *Who was he, really?*

"I'm twenty-eight years old," he began. "I graduated from UC Berkeley with a degree in business. I live in an apartment with my roommate, Dev, who's been a friend of mine since college. He's super funny and smart—an engineer—and he's always there for me. I feel really lucky to have him in my life."

"Linda said you're one of the best Big Brothers our chapter has. What got you into that?" asked Diane.

"My parents are big supporters of Big Brothers Big Sisters. When I heard about the challenges some of these kids have—and what a difference a few hours of your time can make in their lives—I signed up."

"Sounds like you have nice parents," said Diane.

"I do—they're my heroes. I've always looked to them for advice. Dad's a television executive and Mom's a middle-school principal. I have an older brother, Brian, who's in the real estate business. He has his MBA and thinks I should get mine, but I'm not sure that's the direction I want to go in life."

"Why not?" asked Diane.

"I've been thinking about that a lot lately," said Josh. "I don't know if business is where I should be focusing my career. I know I'm not tapping my highest talents in sales."

"What do you love to do?"

"I love talking to people. I don't necessarily love trying to sell them things."

"What bothers you about that?" asked Diane.

"I don't like that sales always ends up with my agenda, wanting them to buy something, whether it's helping them or not. At least that's what it feels like to me."

Diane laughed. "You are a straight shooter, aren't you? That's an interesting perception of what sales is all about. I have to tell you, as a career salesperson, that's not how I feel. I won't push a sale if I don't think it's in the other person's best interest. But I love nothing more than getting the right product or service to the right person."

Talking to Josh, Diane felt some of her old passion for work pumping through her veins again.

Josh shook his head. "Yeah, that's not me. My company has a great product and I know there are people who need and want it. But connecting the two doesn't really ignite my passion."

"Can you think of a time when you *did* feel passionate about working with others?" Diane asked.

"Passionate?"

"An experience that was so engaging you lost track of time."

Josh gave it some thought. "The only thing that comes to mind is from my college days. During my junior and senior years, I took journalism classes and got on the staff of the college newspaper. I was thrilled when they asked me to cover newsworthy events on campus. I got to interview students, faculty, and administrators. It turned out to be so much fun that I couldn't believe I was earning college credit for it. And despite all the extra work on top of my classes, my GPA was going up. I loved it."

"What, in particular, did you love about that?" asked Diane.

"I really enjoyed interviewing people and seeing if I could pull out the relevant details and turn them into a good story."

"Given how much you enjoyed it, why didn't you pursue a degree and career in communications?"

"My father wasn't crazy about the idea. He encouraged me to stick with my business major. He said it would be a lot more lucrative in the real world."

Diane gazed at Josh with a thoughtful expression. "So if I'm hearing you right, it sounds like what you value is friendship and family—and that you have a heart for talking to people and telling their stories."

"That's about right," said Josh. "Maybe that's enough about me. If you don't mind, I'd like to hear more about you."

For a moment, Diane was taken aback. It had been a while since she'd talked about herself.

"Okay," she said. "Following your lead, I'll start with my age. I'm about to turn sixty. My assistant is organizing a big party, but I'm just not all that excited about it."

"Why not?"

"I guess it's because I'm not really sure what I want to do when I grow up, and people at the party are bound to ask me what's next. Let's see—I graduated from USC and married my college sweetheart, Mark. We've enjoyed thirty-five years of married life and have a daughter who has given us two beautiful grandchildren—twins, in fact. That's the only thing I'm sure of—I want to spend more time with the twins."

"You don't really strike me as a full-time grandmother," said Josh. "From what I learned from Linda, your career is really important to you. Is that true?"

"Yes, I love sales. I've loved it from the day I started as a junior sales rep, and if I'm honest, I've loved being vice president of sales for Quest Media. I'm so fortunate to work in a creative industry with so many talented people. But after listening to you, I think I have the opposite issue. You sound like you're understimulated and not crazy about sales. While I love my work, I'm overstimulated and more or less exhausted all the time. The global travel is really getting to me. People keep hearing me complain about it and are suggesting that maybe I should retire."

"Is that what you want to do?" Josh asked.

"You really do like to interview people, don't you? To answer your question, I don't know. I've always valued being productive, and I don't know how I'd feel useful if I retire."

When lunch arrived, their conversation drifted to favorite books, movies, and the things they valued most in life—family, friends, and pets.

As they were finishing, Diane said, "Talking with you, I remembered why I got into this field in the first place. I'm not sure it's the right place to be at this stage of my life, but your questions got me thinking."

Josh smiled. "It's really a privilege to hear someone as successful as you talking about their life. And your questions have given me a lot to think about, too."

"From my viewpoint, this was a good *essence* meeting," said Diane. "I'm interested in pursuing this, but I need to think about how it will work logistically, in terms of my time and priorities. What do you think about moving on to *form* during our next meeting?"

"That sounds great. I was hoping there would be a next meeting."

They stood and walked to the exit. At the door, Josh extended his hand.

"Thank you so much for the time you've given me today," he said.

Diane returned the handshake. "You're welcome. It's been a pleasure—and I'm not just saying that."

ONE MINUTE INSIGHTS

Pause, Reflect, and Learn

- A successful first meeting with a potential mentor or mentee puts the personal before the tactical—or, as Diane says, essence before form. Do your values match? Do your personalities click? Does the conversation flow?
- No matter if you are a mentor looking for a mentee or a mentee looking for a mentor, remember to go with your gut when making decisions about pursuing a mentoring relationship. If it doesn't feel right, it's probably not a good match.
- If you are the potential mentee, remember to thank your potential mentor. No matter what the outcome of the meeting, that person extended a favor to you by considering.

MISSION IMPERATIVE

Over the next ten days, as Diane jetted off to another time zone, Josh and Diane exchanged a couple of e-mails, expressing their mutual interest in their budding mentoring relationship.

When Diane returned from her travels, they met again at the Bayside Grill.

"I've been thinking about the logistics of our mentoring partnership—in other words, how we want to work together," Diane said as they settled into their seats.

"You mean the form part, as opposed to the essence part that we talked about last time?" asked Josh.

"Exactly. From my experience, the first step in any working relationship is to have a clear mission statement. After all, if we don't know where we're going, chances are good we won't get there."

"What exactly do you mean by a mission?" Josh asked.

—

The first step in any working relationship is to have a clear mission statement.

—

"A mission gets at the purpose of our mentoring relationship. While our mission statement doesn't have to be complicated, it should be written with care, because it will be the most important thing we'll agree on together."

"I've heard that a mission statement tells people what business you're in. So what business are we in, Diane?"

"I think we're in the regaining passion business," Diane said with conviction. "How does this sound? 'The mission for our mentoring relationship is to help you regain excitement about what you're up to in the world.'"

"That sounds good," Josh said, "but I think it's missing something. A big issue for me is clearing up my confusion about my career. How about saying 'Our mission is to help me regain clarity about and passion for my work in life'?"

"That sounds good. You do have a way with words."

"Thanks, but the problem I have with that mission statement is that it's all about me. What's in our relationship for you?"

"My mentor, Warren, told me that if I mentored someone else, I'd get the energy and focus I need to pursue my own next steps."

"So you're telling me that helping me is going to help you?" Josh smiled at the thought that he really might have something to offer someone as successful as Diane.

"That's what Warren says—and I've learned to listen to his advice. He also taught me about the power of journaling."

She reached into her briefcase and pulled out a spiral-bound notebook. "This is going to be my mentoring journal. I'm old-school, so paper still works for me. You might want to keep your mentoring journal on your phone or something. This is where we'll keep track of how our mentoring journey is going."

Josh took out his phone and fired up a new app he'd been playing with.

"For now, I'll dictate my notes into this," he said. "Where do I start?"

"The first step is to write down our agreed-upon mission statement."

"Let me repeat it out loud so I can capture it." Josh spoke into his phone: "The mission of our mentoring relationship is to help me regain clarity about and passion for my work in life."

Diane was writing in her journal as Josh spoke. "Right," she said.

"What's next?" asked Josh.

"That depends on what comes up," said Diane. "Our journals are where we'll record your concerns, needs, moments of progress, and ideas for ways I can help you. Warren assures me that in the process I'll be gaining insights and clarity as well."

"I hope so. I like the two-way-street aspect of that," Josh said.

"Now for the rest of this lunch, why don't we address any issues that might be slowing down your progress? For example, you mentioned a concern that the new recruit who is sharing your cubicle is outperforming you."

"I hate to admit it, but it does bother me," said Josh.

"I understand," said Diane. "But in the short run, I recommend you try to learn something from him, as your boss suggested."

"But I'm not even sure I want to continue in sales."

"I understand," said Diane. "But I don't think you should mentally drop out of your present job until you have a clear direction and some potential opportunities. Without a job to pay the bills, thinking about next steps in your career will be hard."

"So I should get my ego out of the way and learn from Eric. I guess that will buy me some time to do some big-picture thinking."

"Precisely," said Diane.

"For me, the hardest part will be swallowing my pride and learning from someone who's younger than I am."

"I'll be eager to hear how that goes. We won't be able to meet face-to-face for a month, because I'm going on another trip."

While they waited for the bill to arrive, Josh and Diane scheduled a phone call for two weeks away.

Putting the phone meeting into her calendar, Diane realized that by the time she and Josh had their next call, she would be sixty years old.

Where do the years go? she wondered.

ONE MINUTE INSIGHTS

Pause, Reflect, and Learn

- Successful mentoring starts with a powerful mission statement. What do you hope to achieve with your partnership? Articulate your mission in a simple statement you can readily call upon.
- While mission statements focus on the mentee, both mentor and mentee will give and receive in the relationship. The mission statement should reflect this.
- Keep a journal of your mentoring journey so that you can track your goals and progress.

TAKE ACTION

MISSION

*Create a mission—
a purpose for your
mentoring partnership.*

ENGAGEMENT: ESTABLISHING THE RELATIONSHIP

Mark Bertman stood at the podium and looked out across a ballroom that was filled with friends, loved ones, and admirers of his wife, Diane. The tables were adorned with balloons and flowers. Across the back wall hung a banner that read: "Happy 60th, Diane! It's Only the Beginning."

Mark raised his champagne glass and tapped it with his fork, sending a clear *ding, ding, ding* across the room.

"May I have your attention, please?" he boomed in his pleasant baritone. "Let's raise our glasses to my fabulous wife, a special person in all our lives. May this year be the beginning of great things to come for you, Diane."

Applause broke out, and the crowd cheered. Warren Riggs toasted Diane next, and several other key people in her life followed suit.

When the toasts were finished, Warren walked over to Diane and pulled her aside for a private moment.

"Happy birthday, you amazing woman, you," he said as he gave her a hug.

Diane hugged him back. "Oh, Warren. I don't know how to even begin to thank you. You've been so important in my life."

"I'm glad I didn't see a retirement banner when I walked in."

"No, you didn't. You'll be proud to know I took your advice. I'm now in a mentoring relationship."

"Congrats! Tell me about it."

"I'm mentoring a twenty-eight-year-old who's working for a software firm. Josh is in sales, but he's not doing very well, in terms of results or satisfaction."

"So how is the mentoring going?"

"I started with the essence and form model you taught me years ago. The essence part was easy. I really like Josh. He's a good guy."

"What makes you say that?"

"For one thing, he's a Big Brother to an at-risk teenager, which tells me he cares about people. He's also polite, candid, and easy to talk to. I think he feels comfortable with me, too."

"What about form?" asked Warren.

"We started that by clarifying a mission statement."

"Excellent!" said Warren. "What's your mission?"

Diane easily recited the mission from memory: "Our mission is to help Josh regain clarity about and passion for his work in life."

"Fantastic. What's next?"

"That's what I was going to ask you! I'm really not clear about where we go from here. I have managed plenty of people and projects at work. But it seems like being a mentor is different."

Decide how you want to communicate with each other—how often and by what means.

"It sounds like you've got a clear mission. But as with any successful relationship, you have to decide how you want to communicate with each other—how often and by what means."

Diane frowned. "Because of my hectic travel schedule, we didn't set up a regular meeting. Maybe that was a mistake. Right now it's catch as catch can."

"You might want to put some structure around that. Make a commitment to a weekly meeting, at least, even if it's on the phone or online. Missing a call is okay once in a while, but early in the relationship—while you're getting it established—I do recommend a weekly check-in."

Diane bristled at another weekly commitment.

Warren saw the displeased look on her face. "Don't worry, Diane, this is only for the first month or so while you're getting to know each other. After that you won't need to be in touch as often."

"Okay, I guess. I know you said that this mentoring thing would be a win-win, and that I would get something out of it, too. But to be honest, so far it feels pretty one-sided. He's fairly young and inexperienced."

"That might be the case. But you'd be surprised—younger people benefit us by introducing us to new ways to think and communicate. For example, I've learned all about taking initiative from you, Diane."

"Really?"

"Absolutely. Watching you take risks over the years inspired me to go for new opportunities as well. But the reason I was open to your ideas was because of how well we engaged together and the trust we built with each other. Hopefully you and Josh can develop that same engagement and trust."

"I hope so, too. I'll keep you informed as we move down the road."

"That's a good idea, because every now and then you'll want to stop and review where you are, and how you're coming along on your mission. I'd love to be a part of that process and help you in any way I can."

Suddenly, they both noticed a minor commotion as a young woman wheeling a two-seat stroller made her way through the crowd to Diane.

"No monopolizing my mom on her birthday!" the woman said to Warren. "The girls and I flew two thousand miles to be with her today."

Diane's eyes grew wide and her face lit up. After giving her daughter, Sarah, a bear hug, she kneeled by the stroller to gaze and coo at her granddaughters.

When Diane looked up, there were tears in her eyes. "This is the best birthday present—ever."

*

For Josh, the two weeks before his next call with Diane were challenging. It was all about ego containment as he tried to learn from his office mate, Eric.

When the day for their call finally came, Josh ducked out of the JoySoft lobby on his lunch break and rang Diane.

"Hello?"

He was surprised how relieved he felt just hearing her voice. "Hi, Diane. It's Josh."

"How's it going?" she asked.

"Remember Eric, my office mate that you and my

boss encouraged me to learn from? He really is good. He's signed on a half-dozen big clients, and now they're giving him his own office. At first I was upset about that, because I have seniority. It seemed like I should be getting a new office before he did. But as I thought about it, why would I push for a new office when I'm not even sure sales is the right field for me?"

—

Once you get clear on
what you really want to
do, all kinds of doors will
open for you.

—

"That's good thinking, Josh. The fact that someone else is succeeding in his career is a good thing, right? Sales is obviously Eric's sweet spot. Once you get clear on what you really want to do, all kinds of doors will open for you as well."

"I hope so. Frankly, it has been a difficult couple of weeks."

"How long has this latest development with Eric been bugging you?"

"I found out about his new office the day after our last talk."

"Why didn't you shoot me an e-mail?"

"Because I knew we had a phone call scheduled, and I wanted to respect your time."

"I appreciate that courtesy, Josh. But if something important comes up that you could use support on, let's agree that you shouldn't wait until the scheduled meeting to get in touch."

"Agreed," said Josh.

"In fact, I was talking to my mentor, Warren, and he recommended that at least for the first month or so, we should stay in touch once a week."

"So it's okay to e-mail or text you with something like this?"

"Actually, for discussing issues I prefer phone calls—perhaps it's a generational thing. But any communication is better than none, particularly if something's bothering you."

"What I'm hearing you say is that in the interest of accomplishing our mission, we need to keep the lines of communication open."

"Exactly," said Diane. "As for e-mails, I'd also like you to send me a short, weekly summary about what is going on with you, what you're thinking about, and how I might help. Don't just dictate your thoughts into that journal app of yours—communicate with *me* as well. Does that sound good?"

"That sounds great," said Josh. "But speaking of how you might help, you've got a lot more experience in sales than Eric does. What I'd really appreciate would be any tools and techniques that could help me become a better salesperson now. I mean, you're a VP of sales, after all."

Diane chose her next words carefully. "I think this is a good time to talk about the difference between mentoring and coaching. I'm your mentor, Josh, not your sales coach. Those two terms are often used interchangeably. But for our purposes, a coach helps you focus on performance and skill development. For example, right now, Eric is a coach of yours. A mentor helps you focus on longer-term issues—things like work-life balance and big-picture career development."

Josh said, "That makes sense, I guess. So what should I be focusing on?"

"Focus on your job during the day, but don't take it with you at night or on weekends. Instead, use that time for introspection. You said your passion is talking to people and telling their stories—what could you be doing outside of work that develops those abilities? Maybe start there."

"If you insist, Mentor."

"I do. But don't be too surprised if every once in a while a good sales tip or two comes out of my mouth."

ONE MINUTE INSIGHTS

Pause, Reflect, and Learn

- Set some ground rules early on for the type of engagement you expect from each other. How often will you meet? Will you call, text, or e-mail between meetings? How frequently?
- In the beginning of the relationship—as mentor and mentee are getting to know each other and building a foundation for their relationship—engagement should be more frequent.
- There's a difference between mentoring and coaching. Coaching is focused on short-term, task-related issues. Mentoring focuses on big-picture, long-term goals.

TAKE ACTION

ENGAGEMENT

*Agree on ways to engage
that work with your
personalities and schedules.*

TAKING TIME FOR INTROSPECTION

The following Monday evening, Josh was commuting home on the freeway, zoning out with his usual, albeit mind-numbing, talk radio. Suddenly, he remembered Diane's advice about using his hours outside of work for introspection. Turning off the noise, he did his best to quiet his mind.

A few miles later he noticed a billboard advertising an online university. As he got closer, he saw that the school offered a master's degree in public relations and communications. His thoughts drifted to the happy times he'd spent working on his school newspaper, interviewing people and writing articles.

"Wait a minute!" he said out loud. "That could be a way forward!"

A degree in communications inspired him much more than the thought of getting an MBA, as his brother had suggested. Since it was an online program, he could also keep his job while he studied.

As soon as he got home, he fired off an e-mail.

Dear Diane,
I can't wait to tell you about what happened to me on the way home today. I think I might have stumbled onto something important. Talk about the power of introspection!
    Would you be able to meet—either in person or on the phone—sometime soon?
    Best,
    Josh

*

Diane's plane touched down in Heathrow Airport and taxied to the gate. She turned on her phone to check her mail and was pleased to see a new e-mail from Josh, who seemed to be taking her advice to be in more regular touch. After reading through it, she jotted a quick reply:

Dear Josh,

I just landed in London, where I've been invited to an emergency board meeting. I don't have all the details yet, but I'm scheduled to be here until Friday. It definitely looks like it's going to be a wild week. I can find time to talk if it's urgent, but if it can wait until next week, I'd prefer to get together face-to-face over lunch at the Bayside Grill on Monday.

    Diane

Josh shot back:

No problem. It sounds like we'll both have news to share! See you Monday.

                    *

Diane sat at a large oval table with the six board members of Quest Media—including the president of the company. Besides Diane, several other top leaders from the company were in attendance, including the vice presidents of finance, operations, and marketing.

This was the first time in her thirty-five years in the industry that she'd attended an emergency board meeting. She was nervous, but also curious.

The chairman of the board, Isaac Rosenthal, kicked it off. "The reason we've invited all of you to this off-site meeting is that we have some concerns about Quest Media's performance. We wanted to speak with and get input from as many of the company's key players as possible."

For the next hour they talked about the fact that while revenues were up, expenses were growing faster than the overall profit margin. Since this trend was not sustainable, the board wanted to hear the thinking from the top management team.

After another hour of discussion, Chairman Rosenthal said, "We've generated some good ideas here. For the next quarter I think all of us need to step back, look at what's happening, and come back with a turnaround plan."

He looked at Diane. "I'm a firm believer that production minus sales equals scrap. As the vice president of sales, you know that as well as anyone, Diane. I've always admired your work ethic and creativity. Since you have the longest tenure with the company and probably know more about the business than anyone else, I'd like you to consider chairing that turnaround planning group."

Outwardly, Diane nodded. Inwardly, she thought: *Why does it always have to be me?*

*

Back at the hotel that evening, Diane pulled her mentoring journal from her briefcase. She needed to write about the mixed feelings she was having. On the one hand, she was flattered that Isaac had singled her out for a leadership role. On the other hand, this would be another time-consuming, long-term commitment.

Her notebook opened to the page where she'd written her mentoring mission to help Josh "regain clarity about and passion for" his work in life. She had to smile. Clearly, she was on the same mission.

She decided to take her own advice and devote the rest of her evening to introspection.

ONE MINUTE INSIGHTS

Pause, Reflect, and Learn

- Taking time for introspection is essential for mentees and mentors alike.
- When was the last time you stopped to zoom out from your life and get a big-picture perspective?
- Set a regular time to think about where you are and where you want to be.
- Writing about issues that arise during introspection can help to clarify them.

SPEAKING YOUR TRUTH

The following Monday, Diane and Josh met at the Bayside Grill for lunch.

"I really appreciate you meeting me today, especially considering that you're just back from a big meeting in London," said Josh.

"I was actually looking forward to our lunch. I've been doing nothing but business meetings for a week and it's great to change the channel. What's this exciting news you have to tell me?" she asked.

"What would you think if I pursued a master's degree in public relations and communications?"

"Where's that idea coming from?" said Diane.

"Believe it or not, I saw the degree advertised on a billboard when I was driving home. I'd just turned off the radio to do some of your recommended introspection and, boom, there it was."

"I remember you saying that you enjoyed the work you did on your college newspaper."

"I really did," said Josh. "What excites me is that it's an online program, so I can pursue my degree while I'm still working. Plus, the cost is pretty manageable. And who knows where it will lead? Maybe I'll become JoySoft's communications director someday."

"I think it's a great idea," said Diane. "Even though there can be no company without sales, communications and PR are critical to any business."

"I was hoping you'd say something like that," said Josh.

"Come to think of it, would you like to talk to the head of our PR department to learn more about the field?"

"That would be great!"

"I suggest you have a talk with your boss to tell her about what you're thinking. From what you told me, I got the impression she wants to help you develop, whether you stay in sales or pursue another job within the company. So it sounds like she'd be supportive of your idea."

"I hope so," said Josh. "So what about you? How was your trip to London?"

"There's a lot happening, and I'm a little overwhelmed, to be honest. I've been asked to head up a big committee to help turn our company around."

"Did you accept the job?" asked Josh.

"No, I didn't. Instead, I took my own advice."

"What advice is that?"

"The advice I gave you about taking time to think and get some perspective. Assuming responsibility and doing it all has been my modus operandi for decades. This time I stopped myself from automatically saying yes, which is what I would have done in the past. I'm taking some time to consider all my options."

"So this mentoring thing is a two-way street after all," said Josh.

"Indeed."

"You suggested I have a talk with my boss to speak my truth about pursuing my master's degree. Forgive me if it's none of my business, but should you be telling your board what you're thinking, too?"

"I should," said Diane.

She smiled and shook her head. "Warren was right. In helping you figure out where you're going, I'm figuring out my next steps."

*

As Josh headed down the hall toward Eva's office, he felt butterflies. But this time, he imagined Diane cheering him on.

Eva was looking at Josh's sales report when he walked in. "Congrats on the uptick in your performance," she said. "How did this happen?"

"I took your advice, swallowed my pride, and started taking some pointers from Eric."

Eva smiled. "I'm glad. Do your improved sales numbers mean you're more enthusiastic about your job?"

"I'm definitely more enthusiastic now that my numbers are going up," Josh said.

"That's great," said Eva.

"But I've been thinking about what you said during my quarterly review."

"What's that?"

"You said that I should either get my numbers up or redirect my career energies, because sales isn't for everybody."

"Tell me more."

Josh cleared his throat. "What do you think about me pursuing an online master's degree in communications?"

Eva sat back in her chair. "A number of JoySoft people have found that furthering their education is beneficial. It does mean that your nights and weekends will no longer be free."

"I realize that, but I think it would enhance my strengths. And who knows? It could make me more valuable to the company."

"Time will tell about that. But you owe it to yourself to find work that inspires you. As long as you can keep your sales numbers up while you study, I'm all for it."

"Thanks for your support," Josh said. "You're a great boss, and I don't take that for granted. As hard as it was to have you point out my poor performance, your guidance has been really helpful to me these last several weeks. I'm even enjoying learning from Eric."

"I must say, Josh, I'm really impressed with your attitude today. It's so different than during the talk we had a couple of months ago. Frankly, I was having some serious concerns about you. I'm so glad you're turning things around."

*

Diane took a deep breath, picked up the phone, and called Isaac Rosenthal, Quest Media's chairman. After a brief hello, she got right to the point.

"I've been thinking about our meeting in London, and the turnaround we've been discussing."

Isaac let out a humorless laugh. "I not only think about it, I lose sleep over it. What are your thoughts?"

"I appreciate your suggestion that I take the lead on the turnaround committee, but I'm not sure I'm up for it at this point."

"What do you mean?"

"Frankly, I think it's more responsibility than I'm willing to take on right now."

Isaac paused before answering. "I'm disappointed, but I appreciate your candor. You're not thinking of retiring, are you?"

"Not entirely, no."

"What are your plans?"

"That's what I'm trying to figure out. But I do know that the role you've laid out for me isn't the one I want to play. I think Larry Zuniga, with his operations mind-set, might be perfect for it. He and I had some great discussions in London."

"Larry?" Isaac sounded intrigued. "That's an interesting idea, Diane. Let me sleep on it."

ONE MINUTE INSIGHTS

Pause, Reflect, and Learn

- As a mentor, encourage your mentee to tell the truth about where they are and what they want. At the same time, tell the truth about where you are and what you want.
- As a mentee, you have observations to offer as well. Don't fall into the trap of letting your mentor always take the lead in conversations.
- Sometimes, just by asking a question, a mentee can make a positive difference in a mentor's life.

LEARNING TO NETWORK

Josh popped his head into Eric's office. "Have a minute?" he asked.

Eric, who'd been about to dial another call, put down his phone. "Sure. Have a seat."

Josh lowered himself into the armless chair next to Eric's desk. Framed motivational quotes—alongside Eric's famous calendar—filled the walls of Eric's private office.

"Still putting those red Xs up, I see," said Josh.

"Yep."

"I actually keep a calendar like that myself now," Josh said. "It helps."

"I know, right? Something about the visual instant gratification. And I noticed your numbers are up. Looks like you've got your mojo back."

"Thanks to the things you coached me to do," Josh said. "I asked for referrals and followed up on them. I made cold calls. I reconnected with clients who haven't bought from us for a while, and I sold deeper into existing accounts."

"Excellent!" said Eric.

"All those things have gotten my numbers up. But I've hit a plateau again. I haven't closed a deal all week. I was wondering if you have any other ideas."

"Only three," said Eric.

"Great. What are they?"

"Prospect, prospect, and prospect—in that order."

Josh was less than enthused by Eric's reply. Apparently it showed on his face.

"You think there's some magic bullet?" said Eric. "No bullet. Just hard work. Everyone you meet is a potential client, man. Your Uber driver. Your Aunt Margaret. The manager at your local electronics store."

Josh wondered about Eric's sweeping generalization. "Everyone?" he asked dubiously.

"Everyone," said Eric, firmly.

*

Josh and Diane's next face-to-face meeting took place in Griffith Park. They'd planned ahead to wear shorts and running shoes.

"Thanks for agreeing to multitask," said Diane. "This is the only exercise I'll be able to squeeze in today. Hope you don't mind if we walk at a fast clip."

"Not at all," said Josh. "According to an article I read, walking meetings increase creativity. My boss, Eva, is all for them."

"Speaking of Eva, did you get a chance to tell her about pursuing your master's degree?"

"Yes. She was supportive and said that as long as I hit my numbers, what I do on my own time is up to me."

"That's good news!" said Diane enthusiastically.

"What about you?" asked Josh. "Are you still feeling overwhelmed? Did you speak with your board chairman?"

"Sort of and yes," answered Diane. "Work is intense, but at least I'm not traveling for a few weeks. And I fessed up about not wanting to lead the turnaround team."

"How'd that go over?"

"Not too badly, especially since I followed some good advice I learned from Warren. He said, 'Diane, if you offer an alternative rather than just flat-out refuse an idea, you'll do well in life.' So far I've found that to be true."

"What was your alternative idea?" Josh asked.

"My alternative is a person. Larry Zuniga. He's been our VP of operations at Quest Media for eight years. He's a real go-getter, with some great new ideas that I think can really help the company right now."

Their conversation died down as the trail became steeper. Below them, the city of Los Angeles stretched out in the distance.

—

Cultivating productive relationships is a major key to success.

—

When they reached the summit, Diane said, "Cultivating productive relationships is a major key to success. Remember when I asked you if you'd like to talk to the head of our corporate PR department?"

"Sure," said Josh.

"I told him about your interest in writing and communications, and he said he'd be happy to spend some time with you. He's an inspiring guy." She reached into the pouch strapped around her waist and pulled out a business card. "He gave me this and said for you to give him a call."

Josh took the card and glanced at the name:

DOUG SHARF
Director of Communications,
Quest Media

*

Josh arrived early for his meeting with Doug. Sitting in the small reception area outside Doug's office, he thought through what he planned to talk about. Informational interviews about a particular career, as he knew, were really about fact-finding—understanding what someone did, why, and then trying to figure out if that type of work suited you.

Doug greeted Josh warmly and ushered him inside.

As Josh sank into an armchair he looked around the office. Framed photographs of California's beautiful Pacific Coast lined the walls. Immediately feeling comfortable, he dove right in.

"Thanks for seeing me today, Doug. I'm really grateful to Diane for connecting us. I can't wait to find out what you do and how you got into this job. As Diane may have told you, I've got a passion for writing and communications, but I'm not using it. I'm eager to learn from successful people who've been able to make a career out of their passions. From what I hear from Diane, you've done that."

"That's high praise, Josh, and I'm not sure I can live up to it. But I'll sure try."

Over the next twenty minutes, Doug described how he'd grown up in a small town in Texas and how he found his way to UCLA for college.

"Why UCLA?" asked Josh.

"I was on the swim team in high school. I always wanted to surf, and I heard California calling me. At UCLA, when I wasn't studying or surfing, I was writing for the college newspaper."

"I wrote for my college newspaper, too," Josh said with enthusiasm. "That's where I learned that I loved to write."

"I can relate," said Doug. "It was that nagging desire to write—combined with a love for business—that got me my first job in the publicity department at a small publishing company."

"How did you end up at Quest?" Josh asked.

"One of the senior managers was a surfing buddy of mine. When an opening came up in the communications department about fifteen years ago, he told me to apply. This is an exciting place. We do cutting-edge, creative work, and our team is incredibly talented. I've loved it from the day I started, and I was fortunate to be promoted to director a couple of years ago."

"What are your day-to-day duties?" asked Josh.

Doug took another fifteen minutes to describe in detail the work he was doing.

"Sounds like a dream job," said Josh.

"It is," said Doug. "The best part is, this whole time I've been able to pursue my love of surfing. There's nothing like catching a wave and feeling the power of the ocean as you're flying toward shore."

"When I hear you talk about surfing, Doug, I can feel your passion. The crazy thing is, when you talk about your career, I feel the same thing. Do you know how lucky you are?"

"You bet I do. I feel grateful every day," said Doug.

"The way you've created a life you love around work and surfing is inspiring. And if what I hear from Diane is true, your enthusiasm has a positive effect on everyone around here. I'll bet when you were a kid from a small town in Texas you never dreamed that one day you'd step onto the campus at UCLA and build a life around your dreams."

"Wow, you're right. I never thought of it that way. You're pretty good at this whole communication thing. Your ability to listen and tell my own life story back to me inspires even me!"

Doug stood up and extended his hand. "It's really been a pleasure."

"Thanks," Josh said.

Suddenly, he remembered one of the motivational sayings on Eric's wall: *Always Be Closing*. Maybe this was a sales opportunity. He could hear Eric's voice in his head, reminding him that everyone was a prospect.

Everyone?

Everyone.

"So, Doug, are you happy with your current software system? I have a number of media clients who use our product, JoySoft, and are finding it really helps them streamline their department's work."

Doug looked chagrined. "Is this a sales pitch?"

Suddenly, Josh realized his mistake.

"I'm sorry—occupational hazard," Josh said. "In my current job I'm supposed to look at everyone as a prospect."

Doug frowned. "I appreciate your enthusiasm, but that's not really what this meeting was about."

"No, I get that," said Josh. "Please forgive my blunder. You've been more than kind to see me today, and I got so much out of your story. I'm really sorry."

"Apology accepted," said Doug. "Don't worry about it."

But Josh did worry about it.

ONE MINUTE INSIGHTS

Pause, Reflect, and Learn

- As a mentor, one of the greatest things you can share with your mentee is your network. Think of people who might be able to support your mentee and help them become acquainted.
- Mentees, don't forget that you have a network as well! Always be thinking of people who might be relevant connections for your mentor, and don't be shy about offering to make introductions.
- Tread lightly on the networks of others. Never use or abuse the connections made for you. Be gracious and respectful to all involved.

TAKE ACTION

NETWORKING

Expand your network with that of your mentor or mentee.

BUILDING TRUST

Josh called Diane immediately after his interview with Doug. When his call went straight to voice mail, he sent a text:

> Thanks again for introducing me to Doug Sharf. I
> need to update you. It's important. Do you have time
> to meet?

They arranged to get together over coffee the next day.

*

"You said it was important," said Diane as she walked into the coffee shop with Josh. "What's up?"

"You trusted me with one of your colleagues—and I blew it."

"What happened?"

"Doug was great, and his story was really inspiring. Everything was fine until the end of our meeting. I kept hearing Eric's voice in my head telling me to 'Always Be Closing,' and how everyone's a prospect. Before I knew it, I was more or less pitching him on some software. I'm really sorry, Diane. The last thing I wanted to do was offend him."

"Thank you for telling me about this. But Doug already called me."

Josh's shoulders slumped. "Oh, jeez."

"Want to know what he said?"

"I can only imagine. But go ahead."

"He waxed on about his great conversation with you, talking about what a talented young man you appeared to be and how your thoughtful questions made him reflect on an important period of his life."

"Really?"

"Yes. He did tell me that right when you were about to leave, you almost started selling him on some software. But he said you apologized immediately and even sent him a nice note."

Josh let out a sigh of relief. "Still, I won't blame you if you don't trust me with your other contacts anytime soon."

"On the contrary, I trust you even more after this," Diane said matter-of-factly.

"How so?"

—

Everybody makes mistakes.
It's how a person handles
those mistakes that makes
them trustworthy or not.

—

"Everybody makes mistakes. It's how a person handles those mistakes that makes them trustworthy or not. You handled this by promptly admitting your error and apologizing for it—both to Doug and to me."

"I wish I hadn't made the mistake in the first place."

Diane smiled. "Welcome to the human race. Now, tell me about your weekend. How's everything going?"

"Things are going well. I started my first class toward my online master's degree, so I studied pretty much all of Saturday. But I made time on Sunday to go bike riding with Ricky."

"Ricky—your Little Brother in the Big Brothers Big Sisters program?"

"Right. Speaking of which, I heard a rumor that Linda might be leaving the organization. Do you know anything about that?"

"No," said Diane.

"I hope it's not true, because we'd all miss her. She's the best."

"Mark and I are going to the annual fund-raiser this Friday. I'll ask her then. Will you be there?"

Josh shook his head. "Have to study, I'm afraid. But tell Linda I said hello."

ONE MINUTE INSIGHTS

Pause, Reflect, and Learn

- Tactful honesty in a mentoring relationship builds trust.
- Mentoring relationships don't come without challenges. When they arise, build trust by keeping the lines of communication open.
- Mistakes happen; it's how you handle them that builds trust. Admit your part in any mistake and apologize, if appropriate.

TAKE ACTION

TRUST

*Build and maintain trust
with your mentoring partner
by telling the truth,
staying connected, and
being dependable.*

NETWORKING DONE RIGHT

On Friday evening, the sun was just beginning to set as Diane stared out her office window.

"Penny for your thoughts."

She turned to see her husband, Mark, standing in the doorway.

"My thoughts? I was just remembering the first time I saw this view—and how lucky it made me feel."

"You don't feel lucky anymore?" he asked.

"Yes, but about different things, like you and the grandkids."

"Does this mean you're coming close to hanging up your hat here at Quest?"

Diane stood up and began to gather her things. "I don't know. In the few days since Larry Zuniga has stepped up to head our turnaround team, I've been feeling lighter than ever. It's interesting. The act of letting go of power—or is it letting go of responsibility?—feels surprisingly wonderful."

Mark walked over and helped Diane with her coat. "That's a good thing, right?"

"I suppose. But what do I hold on to? Besides you, I mean. What do I do next?"

Mark looked at his watch. "I don't know about the long term, but for now I suggest you come downstairs, hop in the car, and go to Linda's annual fund-raiser with me. We're on the verge of running late."

*

Diane and Mark arrived at the Hilton with just enough time to settle at their table and meet their dinner mates before the program began. That's when Linda Partridge took the podium, gave the audience a warm welcome, and thanked everyone for attending.

"Those of you who aren't familiar with our organization have a treat in store tonight," Linda said. "For more than one hundred years, Big Brothers Big Sisters has operated under the belief that every child has the inherent ability to succeed and thrive in life."

I couldn't agree more, thought Diane.

"As the nation's largest donor- and volunteer-supported mentoring network, Big Brothers Big Sisters makes meaningful, monitored matches between adult volunteers—we call them 'Bigs'—and youth ages six to eighteen—we call them 'Littles'—in communities across the country. As you'll hear later in our program, we develop positive relationships that have a direct and lasting effect on the lives of young people."

Suddenly Linda had Diane's full attention. Although the focus was different, in some ways the work done by Big Brothers Big Sisters was similar to the mentoring she was doing with Josh. She listened with renewed interest.

"Tonight we're going to hear from a Big and Little pair whose mentoring relationship changed both of their lives for the better."

Linda introduced Fran, a middle-aged woman, and Toni, her teenage "Little."

Looking quite grown-up in a knee-length dress and a touch of lipstick, the teenager stepped up to the microphone.

"When I was two years old, my father left our family," Toni began. "By sixth grade I was hanging with the gang boys. They're the guys I grew up with; that's the life I knew. I was kicked out of school for using drugs in seventh grade. I had a bad temper—I was mad at everyone and everything. I hated myself." Her voice faltered.

Fran, Toni's "Big," stepped up and put her arm around the girl.

Toni cleared her throat and went on. "Then I met Fran." The girl turned and gave her mentor a quick smile. "She made me feel good about myself. She really listened to me. When I was interested in trying to do something, Fran helped me make it happen. Last year I graduated from middle school with honors, and in August I graduated as a private in the Young Marines summer program."

The audience broke into applause.

Fran, Toni's Big, kept her remarks short. "I was about Toni's age when my father died, so I know how it feels to be a teenager without a dad. All I can say is, my life is infinitely better with Toni in it. She's taught me to appreciate what I have, and to see the world with new eyes each day. As far as I'm concerned, we're buddies for life."

To her surprise, Diane's eyes filled with tears. Fran and Toni's mentoring relationship was far more personal than the mentorship she had with Josh, and it got to her on a deep level.

As the formal program ended, Linda returned to the podium.

"As a few of you already know, this will be my last event as your program president. After five wonderful years, I've decided it's time for me to step down. I can't tell you what an honor it has been to be a part of this organization. Thank you all for your support, which I hope will continue after I leave."

So the rumor is true, Diane thought.

She and Mark joined the audience in giving another rousing round of applause. Linda left the stage, and the room filled with conversation as dinner was served.

During dessert and coffee, Diane found her way over to Linda's table. They hugged hello, and Linda insisted that Diane sit and chat for a while.

"Have they found your replacement yet?" Diane asked.

"She's irreplaceable!" cried one of Linda's tablemates. "She's going to leave a hole in this organization big enough to drive a tank through."

"No one is irreplaceable," said Linda. "And as much as I've loved my time here, I'm ready for a change."

"I know what you mean," said Diane.

Later, Linda pulled her aside. "Diane, ever since our last lunch I've been thinking. If you're really considering a change, you should think about stepping into my role. We only have an interim replacement. The board would fall all over themselves to have someone with your experience and talent at the helm. And I think it would be an amazing way for you to *refire*—not retire. To move from success to significance, so to speak."

Diane was taken aback. It had never even occurred to her to help run a nonprofit. But talk about being able to give back and enjoy emotional fulfillment! She'd had to fix her mascara after Toni and Fran's presentation tonight, after all.

"It's true that I'm not ready to retire quite yet. But frankly, I don't know what to say."

"Then don't say anything," Linda said. "Just think about it."

On the way home in the car that night, Diane told Mark about her conversation with Linda.

"President of the local chapter of Big Brothers Big Sisters? It's an interesting idea," he said. "If it can get you off the road and give you fulfillment, I say go for it!"

ONE MINUTE INSIGHTS

Pause, Reflect, and Learn

- Cultivate and nurture the important relationships within your network.
- Your mentoring relationship will bring you new perspectives and ideas.
- Whether you're a mentor or a mentee, stay alert and open to the new opportunities that arise through your mentoring experience.

SHARING OPPORTUNITIES

Six months later, Diane had the opportunity to share what she'd learned about mentoring to a wide audience. She was sitting in front of a microphone in the tiny sound room of KBLX, the local affiliate of a popular national radio network. Sitting across the console was the host of the show, Brandy Aston.

Brandy smiled at Diane and read into the microphone:

"From Plato and Aristotle; to Mahatma Gandhi and Martin Luther King; to Benjamin Graham and Warren Buffet, mentorships have been empowering people for thousands of years. Welcome, everyone; I'm Brandy Aston, and today I'll be talking to Diane Bertman, the president of the Los Angeles chapter of Big Brothers Big Sisters, to find out what mentoring is, why it's increasingly popular, and what it can do for you. Good afternoon, Diane."

"Good afternoon," she said.

"So why should somebody be a mentor?" Brandy asked.

—

**The leadership skills you
learn as a mentor can
make you more valuable to
your employer.**

—

"Well, Brandy, the reasons are many. For one thing, the leadership skills you learn as a mentor can make you more valuable to your employer. The research backs this up. A recent study showed that managers who were also mentors were promoted six times more often than those who were not."

"I know mentoring has been helpful in my career," said Brandy. "What about yours? You became a top salesperson at one of the largest media conglomerates in the country. What role did mentoring play in your career?"

"From early on I was fortunate to have a wonderful mentor, Warren Riggs. He taught me about creating a mission for my career. He also showed me how to connect with people and build productive relationships with them."

"That sounds ideal."

"I was fortunate. I'm also privileged to be mentoring to a young man early in his career—and that's also having a positive impact on my life."

"How so?"

"In the course of helping him find his passion, I found mine again."

"That's wonderful!" said Brandy. "Tell me about him."

"At the time we met he was struggling in his job as a sales rep. Today he's motivated at work and pursuing a master's degree. He's working on finding and developing his strengths."

"Sounds like your mentoring has had quite an impact on him."

—

Thousands of case studies clearly demonstrate the power of the mentor-mentee relationship.

—

"Once a person makes the decision to be mentored, they become a partner in unlocking their own potential. Whether it's mentoring new hires, peer-to-peer mentoring, or adult-to-adolescent mentoring, there are thousands of case studies that clearly demonstrate the power of the mentor-mentee relationship."

"You must have a real sense of satisfaction that your mentoring has made a difference in someone's life."

"I do, but what's really amazing is the way my mentee has contributed to my life. You see, I met Josh through our mutual friend, Linda Partridge, who used to hold my job as the president of the L.A. chapter of Big Brothers Big Sisters. Josh has been a Big Brother for several years, and his knowledge about the organization was very helpful to me when I stepped into Linda's old position."

"So the benefits of mentoring can go both ways—or across generations, as you said."

"Absolutely," Diane replied.

"Okay, let's say I want to be a mentor. How do I start?"

"That depends on what type of mentoring you're interested in. If you want to make a difference in the life of a young person, calling up an organization like Big Brothers Big Sisters is a great place to start. If you're interested in professional mentoring, many corporations have or are developing formal mentorship programs. If your company doesn't have a formal program yet, you can start one."

"How?" asked the host.

"The best place to begin is with your HR department head, who will likely be supportive of the idea and spearhead a lot of the organization and legwork. In brief, it involves finding employees who are interested in a mentoring partnership, and then matching people up. It's also important to provide key guidelines about what works—and what doesn't. Finally, it's helpful to offer a check-in system to make sure the mentoring partnerships are working well."

"What if you don't feel like you have the aptitude or training to be a mentor?"

"For mentoring young people, you don't need formal training. Just having a caring heart and carving out some time for that person is all that matters. And for mentoring professional peers, just be willing to take some time away from your work every so often. You'll be surprised how much you already know—and how much you will learn by mentoring others."

For the next twenty minutes, Diane continued to answer Brandy's questions, covering a full range of topics: the importance of a mutually agreed-upon mission statement; how to solidify the relationship through engagement; the right and wrong way to take advantage of a mentor's networking connections; the importance of building trust; how to create and pursue opportunities for each other; and how to keep track of progress.

It felt like they were just getting warmed up when Diane heard bumper music through her headphones—Brandy's cue to end the interview.

"We're at the end of our show," said Brandy, "but I want to thank you, Diane Bertman, for joining me today. I'm sure your thoughts and insights have been helpful to our listeners. And to our audience, thank you for tuning in. I'm Brandy Aston, your host on KBLX Headlines. Until tomorrow, enjoy the sun, everyone."

Brandy waited a beat, removed her headphones, and gave Diane a smile. "You did great," she said.

"Thanks, it was a pleasure. Just for giggles, how many people listen to your show?"

"Not really sure, but the podcast gets about half a million downloads a month."

"Podcasts?" Diane asked, before catching herself and remembering that her daughter, Sarah, listened to them all the time when she was out jogging with the twins in their stroller.

"Our podcasts are quite popular," Brandy asserted. "In fact, we're hoping to expand our broadcasting with a business segment. Some new grants that came in this year are allowing us to build an amazing team. We're just getting started."

"Did you say a business segment?" Diane said.

"Yes. Business advice is usually the most popular topic in our daily radio show."

The gears in Diane's brain started turning.

Was this the type of job Josh might like someday? He loved to tell stories, and he loved to interview people.

She could easily see him creating content for a show like this.

"You said you're just getting started. I'm mentoring a talented young man who's working toward his master's degree in public relations and communications. I know he has to do a master's thesis and maybe he could help create content for your listeners. Would you be willing to talk to him?"

"I'd love to," said Brandy.

*

When Diane got home, her first thought was to give Josh a call about her discussion with Brandy. But she already had a voice-mail message from Josh:

> Diane, great job on the radio interview! Did I really help you find your passion again? Give me a call when you have a minute.

Diane rang Josh's number and he picked right up.

"Thanks for your voice mail," she said. "Yes, you really did help me find my passion. As I was coming home from the radio interview, I was reflecting on the fact that our mentee-mentor relationship has grown into cross-generational mentoring. It really has been a win-win relationship."

"I agree. Without you, I never would have survived at JoySoft or pursued my master's degree."

"Speaking of your master's degree, after our interview, Brandy mentioned that KBLX will be expanding their broadcasting with a business segment. I got the bright idea that maybe your master's thesis could focus on helping them create content for the segment."

"What a great idea! I'm at the point in my program where they're asking me to identify a thesis topic."

"Okay, I'll arrange a time for you and Brandy to talk. But first, it might be a good idea to update your boss."

＊

"Ready?"

Josh looked up to see his boss, Eva, and felt a rush of excitement. Again, he noticed how different he felt than he did before that infamous performance review of so many months ago.

"Ready," he answered.

In Eva's office, Josh updated her about his master's degree program and his thesis focus on creating content for a new business segment at KBLX.

"You know, Josh, even though you continue to keep your sales numbers up, you seem to be more excited about your studies in communications than you are about your work in sales."

"Is it that obvious?"

"Yes, it is. And I was thinking—would you like to speak with the head of our communications department? I was talking to him recently and he's planning to expand his department. This could be a great opportunity for you—even though it might be a loss for me."

Josh looked puzzled. "Thanks."

"I can tell by the look on your face that you're surprised I'd recommend you to another department. What you have to understand is that I've been with this company for many years. During that time I've learned two things. First, what's good for the company is good for me. Second, if we don't help talented young people like you develop your careers within our company, we risk you taking your talent somewhere else."

ONE MINUTE INSIGHTS

Pause, Reflect, and Learn

- There are many different types of mentoring opportunities. Here are a few:
  - **New-Hire Mentoring:** Many organizations have developed formal mentoring programs for newly hired employees. The concept is simple: pair up a new hire with an old hand, and watch the new hire learn and grow.
  - **Peer-to-Peer Mentoring in a Company Context:** These mentoring programs pair peers within an organization to mentor each other.
  - **Cross-Generational Mentoring:** This involves two people from different generations pairing up for mutual benefit and growth. Often a mentor-mentee relationship grows into a cross-generational mentorship.
  - **Adult-to-Adolescent Mentoring:** Organizations like Big Brothers Big Sisters pair adults with youth to give them role models and positive guidance.
- No matter what type of mentoring you're engaged in, it's a great idea to share your experience with others, so they can learn about the benefits.

TAKE ACTION

OPPORTUNITY

*Create opportunities for your
mentee or mentor to grow.*

REVIEW AND RENEWAL

For the rest of the year Josh and Diane met regularly, if a little less often. On the anniversary of their first meeting, they convened as usual at the Bayside Grill.

"It's hard to believe it's been a whole year since we first met," Josh said as he looked around the dining room. "And look at all that's happened."

"I haven't had such a big year in ages," Diane agreed.

"What's on our agenda today?"

"Back when we started this mentorship, we said that at the year-end mark we'd check in to see where we are. That's what I'd like to do today."

Diane pulled a business card from her wallet and handed it to Josh.

"Remember this?"

Josh fingered the card. Printed in small black letters, it read:

Mentoring Mission Statement
To help Josh regain clarity about
and passion for his work in life.

"You laminated it?" he said with a laugh.

"Absolutely," Diane said. "I thought it would make a nice year-end gift for you. This way it won't get dog-eared."

—

You'll never get where you
want to go if you don't
create a mission
statement—and you'll
never know you've arrived
if you don't do regular
reviews.

—

"That's the advantage of having an electronic copy," Josh said with a wink. He pulled out his phone, opened an app, and showed Diane the mission statement on his screen. "The edges don't get frayed."

"Fair enough," said Diane with a laugh.

"So is today going to be like an annual performance review?" asked Josh.

"Sort of," said Diane. "Remember when I told you you'll never get where you want to go if you don't create a mission statement? Well, you'll never know you've arrived if you don't do regular reviews. Today I'd like to see where we stack up against our original goal."

"Makes sense," said Josh.

"So do you think we've done it? Has our mentoring partnership helped you regain clarity and passion for your work in life?"

"No doubt, the answer is yes." He repeated the word, louder this time. "Yes, yes, and YES! Not only am I about to get my master's degree, but I've transitioned from sales into the communications department of JoySoft. I love my new job. I'm doing a lot of writing and creative brainstorming. It hardly feels like working."

"Congratulations. You're proving something I've said for a long time: if you love what you're doing, you'll never have to work a day in your life."

"Diane, I just want to thank you. Doing work I love has been one of the greatest things to come out of our mentorship."

"That makes me feel great. What I didn't expect— even though Warren warned me this would happen—was that I'd be changed by our partnership as well."

"In a good way, I hope," said Josh.

"Absolutely. Rather than stepping down from Quest—and being bored as all get-out—I feel passion for my career again. Being chapter president of Big Brothers Big Sisters brings new meaning to my work and allows time for important things, like my granddaughters."

"That's pretty cool," said Josh. "I'm glad I'm not the only one who's benefited from our time together."

"But think of all you've done," Diane said. "You went from being a burned-out salesperson with bumpy performance reviews to a solid performer on your team. And during that process, you gained clarity about where you want your career to go, and now you're off and running."

"It's true," Josh said. "I mean, in some ways it would've been easy to up and leave JoySoft when the going got tough—especially when I started to realize I didn't see a future in sales. But staying and bringing my sales numbers up helped me gain the confidence I needed to change my focus and transition to our communications department."

"So what's next?" asked Diane.

"I'm not sure. But I don't feel like I'm ready to be mentorless. Can we re-up for another year?"

"That's one of the things I was going to talk to you about—whether or not you wanted to renew our partnership."

"I do!" said Josh.

"Then I'd say a celebration is in order."

As if on cue, the server appeared with two glass flutes, filled nearly to the rims with a golden, bubbling beverage.

Josh's eyes grew wide.

"Wow, Diane—I normally don't drink alcohol in the middle of the day."

"Don't worry," Diane said as she raised her glass. "It's sparkling pear cider from a famous French orchard. No alcohol, but just as festive looking as champagne, I think."

Josh clinked her glass and took a sip. "And even more delicious!"

ONE MINUTE INSIGHTS

Pause, Reflect, and Learn

- Review is an essential part of the mentoring process. You won't know if you've reached your goals unless you look back to see how far you've come.
- Remember to celebrate! Mentoring requires effort. Don't forget to toast to all you've accomplished.
- Some mentoring relationships continue for years, while others take place over a finite period. Talk with your mentee or mentor about what's right for your relationship.

TAKE ACTION

REVIEW AND RENEWAL

*Schedule a regular time to
review progress and renew
your mentoring partnership.*

MENTORING
NEVER ENDS

Two years later, Diane was working in her office at Big Brothers Big Sisters when she got a call from an old friend.

"Warren!" Diane said, recognizing his voice immediately. "Great to hear from you. I was just sitting here thinking about how much I'm enjoying my role as chapter president of this organization. And I owe it all to you."

"You do? How so?"

"If you hadn't pushed me into being a mentor, I'd probably still be traveling nonstop for Quest Media or bored out of my mind in retirement. But thanks to you pushing me to mentor someone else, I was able to find the right path for this stage in my own journey. Just as you said I'd do."

"I'm glad to hear that. Speaking of your mentoring relationship, how's Josh doing?"

"Amazingly well. Once he landed in the communications department of his company, he really began to shine. He was quickly promoted to a manager role. These days he's so engaged in his projects, he tells me he's confused about the difference between work and play."

"That's great news. And what about you, Diane? Is there anything on your mind you want to talk about?"

—

A mentor for one phase of your life may not be the person you need at another point.

—

"As a matter of fact, yes, I do have a question. I've been mentoring Josh for over three years now. We're not meeting as frequently as in the beginning, of course, but I think he still considers me his mentor. What do we do next?"

"Excellent question," said Warren. "And I wish I could give you a definitive answer. But I'm afraid the answer lies within the two of you."

"Tell me more," said Diane.

"For some people, the mentoring relationship is never really over. After all, you and I are going on—what—thirty-five years?"

Diane laughed. "I see your point."

"For others, the mentoring partnership takes place within a specific window of time. Once the mission is accomplished, the mentor and mentee move on."

"That makes sense. People change and grow. I can see how a mentor for one phase of your life may not be the person you need at another point."

"That's right," said Warren. "But one thing's for sure. Everyone needs a mentor—and everyone needs to be mentored."

*

Josh sat at his desk and stared at his computer screen with an eager look on his face. He could remember a time when he dreaded the work in front of him. Now, as he scanned the e-mails in his in-box, he felt excitement about the projects they represented. As he was deciding which one to open first, a subject line caught his eye:

Mentoring Relationship?

He saw from the sender's address that it was from someone in the company, but he didn't recognize the name.
Curious, he clicked open the e-mail. It read:

Dear Josh:
You don't know me but I believe you know my friend,
Eric Aguilar, who used to share an office with you.
He told me about your transition from sales to your
current position as a manager in the communications
department. He shared how you worked with a
mentor who helped you find your passion.

I'm in the finance department and enjoying my
role, but to be honest with you, I don't see a clear
career path for me here.

I don't want to be so presumptuous as to think
you're looking for a mentee. However, it's clear that
you've succeeded in finding your career groove. Eric
says you're a great person and he admires you no
end. I'm hoping you can at least point me in the right
direction as I try to figure out how to move forward.

Thanks for your consideration. If this is of any
interest to you, please send me a reply or feel free to
call me at the number below.
Chris Singer
Ext. 2827

After a moment's thought, Josh gave Chris a call.

"I just got your mentoring request," he said after introducing himself. "And I'm interested in meeting. Any friend of Eric's can't be all that bad."

Chris laughed. "Is that a yes?"

"It's a little premature for that. We have a step or two to go through before we'll know we want to work together. But yes, I'd like to explore this."

"Thanks so much! That's really nice of you. I'm at a loss to know how to return the favor."

"I don't need you to return any favors. But I do have a request."

"What's that?"

"If we develop a mentoring relationship and it's helpful to you, my request is that someday you will pay it forward and ..."

BECOME A MENTOR

PART II

THE MENTOR MODEL

We hope you learned some valuable lessons in our story about mentoring. In this section, we'll recap the action steps that we highlighted after certain sections of the book. Sharp-eyed readers may have noticed that these steps spell out the word MENTOR.

Mission
Engagement
Network
Trust
Opportunity
Review and Renewal

Let's drill down into each of these steps to find out how and why they work.

M = MISSION

TAKE ACTION:
It is essential to create a vision and purpose for your future mentoring partnership.

Sound bite:
The first step in any working relationship is to have a clear mission statement.

Things to remember:

- It is important to find a mentor or mentee who shares your key values.
- Approach a prospective mentor or mentee with courtesy and respect. Regardless of the outcome, thank them for their time.
- Develop a short mission statement to set your intention and direct the mentor/mentee relationship.
- Mentoring adds value on both sides—mentees have knowledge and ideas to offer mentors as well.

E = ENGAGEMENT

TAKE ACTION:

Agree on ways to engage that work for your personalities and schedules.

Sound bite:

Make a commitment to regular meetings, at least, even if they are virtual.

Things to remember:

- Determine the type of engagement that works best for your personalities. Is your mentor or mentee an extrovert or an introvert? Are they best with set times scheduled far in advance? Or do they prefer off-the-cuff e-mails and calls?
- Mentoring partnerships require both the flexibility to engage in digital communication and the power of in-person meetings when possible.

N = NETWORKING

TAKE ACTION:

Expand your network with that of your mentor or mentee. But remember: tread carefully on the networking contacts of your mentoring partner.

Sound bite:

Cultivating productive relationships is a major key to success.

Things to remember:

- Networking is a two-way street—your mentor or mentee can broaden your connections.
- It is essential to tread carefully on the network or contacts of your mentoring partner.
- Networking is not just about one-to-one connections with your mentoring partner's contacts. The one-to-many connections—like those on social media—can be valuable as well.

T = TRUST

TAKE ACTION:

Build and maintain trust with your mentoring partner by telling the truth, staying connected, and being dependable.

Sound bite:

Building trust takes time—and it can be destroyed in an instant.

Things to remember:

- As a mentoring relationship deepens, trust should deepen as well.
- Address communication breakdowns right away, to keep them from eroding trust.
- Honesty and clear communication with your mentoring partner can deepen trust and take your relationship to the next level.

O = OPPORTUNITY

TAKE ACTION:
Create opportunities for your mentee or mentor to grow.

Sound bite:
As a mentoring partner, you'll have access to personal and business opportunities that simply aren't available to non-mentors and non-mentees.

Things to remember:

- A mentoring partnership is a two-way street—both partners have opportunities to bring to the table.
- Mentoring between generations—also known as cross-generational mentoring—is a powerful way to create opportunities by exchanging time-tested and new knowledge.
- Digital media makes potential networks bigger than ever, allowing for more opportunities for mentors and mentees.

R = REVIEW AND RENEWAL

TAKE ACTION:
Schedule a regular time to review progress and renew your mentoring partnership.

Sound bite:
You'll never get where you want to go if you don't create a mission statement—and you'll never know you've arrived if you don't do regular reviews.

Things to remember:

- Scheduling a regular review—once a year, for example—keeps both mentor and mentee on track.
- Ensure that reviews take place by putting them into your calendar when you create your mission statement.
- If your review reveals that the mission has not been accomplished, discuss new strategies to achieve the goal.

CREATING A MENTORING PROGRAM IN YOUR ORGANIZATION

Many companies have discovered that formal mentoring programs can help employees be more successful within the organization. These internal mentoring programs have many benefits for the company as well: more highly trained employees, increased engagement, decreased turnover, and leadership development, to name just a few. As a result, corporate mentoring programs are popping up everywhere.

If you are interested in helping your organization set up a mentoring program, here are a few things to keep in mind.

1. **Start with your Human Resources department.** If you work at an organization large enough to have an HR department, it should be your first stop in discussing the idea. Has the idea been considered before? Is the HR team amenable to spearheading the effort? What support can you provide as the program develops? If you can get your HR department people excited about the idea, you'll be able to rely on their expertise in setting up the program. This usually entails finding employees who are interested in a mentoring partnership and then matching people up.

2. **Teach mentors and mentees the MENTOR model.** Many times potential mentors are scared off mentoring because they think they don't know enough, when in reality the opposite is likely true. Life experience is one of the greatest predictors of a successful mentor, and most mentors find they have that in spades. In this book we've touched on the most essential elements of mentoring, which are summarized in the MENTOR model. These include:

- Crafting a mutually agreed upon **mission** statement
- Solidifying the relationship through **engagement**

- Appropriately taking advantage of a mentor's **networking** connections.
- Building **trust**
- Creating and pursuing **opportunities** for each other
- **Reviewing and renewing** the mentoring relationship on a regular basis

Teach employees to do these six things and they will be well on their way to having dynamic and powerful mentoring relationships.

3. **Establish essential guidelines.** Mentoring can only reach its maximum potential if a regular system of checks and balances is in place. Diane and Josh developed their own process, but within a company environment it's a good idea for all mentoring partnerships to follow the same general guidelines. Set parameters around such items as:

- Frequency of meetings between mentor and mentee
- Timelines of the overall mentoring partnership
- Dates of reviews between mentor and mentee

Putting in the work to create a formal mentoring program is one of the smartest investments an organization can make. Not only does mentoring educate and revitalize people within the organization, it also preserves and expands critical corporate knowledge. With approximately ten thousand people turning sixty-five years old every day, a formal mentoring program can also be a good strategy for transferring older employees' knowledge and skills to the younger members of the workforce.

COACHING VERSUS MENTORING

People are often confused about the difference between coaching and mentoring, mainly because one of the functions of a good mentor is to coach a protégée or mentee.

Like mentoring, coaching is a one-to-one process. But the relationship between an individual and a coach has very specific objectives and goals focused on developing potential, improving relationships, and enhancing performance.

Although mentors utilize coaching skills to serve the mentee, mentoring involves additional tasks, which can include:

- **Being a role model** – displaying specific activities and behaviors that are role specific

- **Consulting** – sharing information about the industry, company, or business unit that the mentor believes is relevant to mentee
- **Brokering** – making introductions to powerful, influential, and otherwise useful individuals in the industry or organization
- **Advocating** – for a mentee's work assignments or career development, to help the mentee's growth and development

Any good mentor will use a coaching process and coaching skills to help the mentee:

- Be clear about big-picture career goals
- Identify and develop leadership qualities
- Develop sound structures and accountability to accomplish the important long-term development goals (vs. the urgent performance ones)
- Understand their own value and needs
- Leverage their best qualities and talents

Coaching skills are refined communication skills combined with an intense service orientation. Training formal or informal mentors in the coaching process and the use of coaching skills has been shown to:

- Reduce turnover
- Increase innovation
- Improve team spirit and loyalty
- Increase productivity

Since 2000, Blanchard Coaching Services has been passionate about making business coaching easy and affordable for people who want and need it. For more information, please call +1 760.739-6967 or visit www. coaching.com.

ACKNOWLEDGMENTS

As we said in the introduction, successful people do not reach their goals alone. Over the course of our lives we've had some great mentors.

Ken would like to acknowledge and give praise to some of his key mentors:

Norman Vincent Peale, for teaching him what true faith was all about; Paul Hersey, for encouraging him to write; Warren Ramshaw and Don McCarty, for guiding him through his graduate studies; Ted and Dorothy Blanchard, for teaching him about love and serving others; Sandy Blanchard, for compelling him to always be his best; Scott and Debbie Blanchard, for teaching him about his leadership and how he can help people win; Paul Ryan, for pushing him to be his best through

[**149**]

basketball; Tony Robbins, for teaching him about the power of your mind and the thoughts you put into it; Pat Lencioni, Tommy Spaulding, and Jon Gordon, for being open to Ken's experience and wisdom and in the process teaching him what they had learned.

Claire would like to acknowledge and give praise to:

Laura Selznick and Carolyn Springer, who walked her through the early years of finding her place in a world of opportunities; Pamela Hartigan, Sammy Ikua, Sally Osberg, Jeff Skoll, and John Wood, who served as guiding lights on the road to social entrepreneurship; Biz Stone and the team at Twitter, for opening the doors to Silicon Valley and teaching her about a then-new world; Bob Goff, Nancy Duarte, Adam Grant, Pam Slim, and Greg McKeown, for setting purposeful entrepreneurial examples to lean into; Anne Lamott, Martha Lawrence, and Don Miller, for thoughts on writing, near and far; Ken Blanchard, for teaching her what it means to serve others with your own success; Barbara and Lance Williams, for many things, but mostly, the burritos.

We'd also like to thank our editors, Henry Ferris, Martha Lawrence, and Renee Broadwell; our agents, Richard Andrews and Esther Fedorkevich; Alais L. M. Griffin, general counsel at Big Brothers Big Sisters of America;

Margery Allen, Ken's executive assistant, right arm and truth teller; and all the sharp-eyed readers at the Skaneateles Country Club.

Finally, we'd like to thank our spouses, Margie Blanchard and Jose Diaz-Ortiz, for always being there for us.

ABOUT THE AUTHORS

Ken Blanchard, one of the most influential leadership experts in the world, is the coauthor of the iconic best seller *The One Minute Manager* and 60 other books whose combined sales total more than 21 million copies. His groundbreaking works have been translated into more than 27 languages, and in 2005 he was inducted into Amazon's Hall of Fame as one of the top 25 best-selling authors of all time.

Dr. Ken Blanchard is also the cofounder and chief spiritual officer of The Ken Blanchard Companies®, an international management training and consulting firm that he and his wife, Margie Blanchard, began in 1979 in San Diego, California. In addition to being a renowned speaker and consultant, Ken is also cofounder of Lead Like Jesus, a worldwide organization committed to helping people become servant leaders. He occasionally serves as a visiting lecturer at his alma mater, Cornell University, where he is a trustee emeritus of the Board of Trustees.

In addition to appearing in major television and print news sources such as the *Today* show, *BusinessWeek*, the *Wall Street Journal*, and many others, Ken has received numerous awards and honors for his contributions in the fields of management, leadership, and speaking. The National Speakers Association awarded him its highest honor, the Council of Peers Award of Excellence. He was inducted into the HRD Hall of Fame by *Training* magazine and Lakewood Conferences, and he received the Golden Gavel Award from Toastmasters International. Ken also received the Thought Leadership Award for continued support of work-related learning and performance by ISA—The Association of Learning Providers.

When he's not writing or speaking, Ken teaches students in the Master of Science in Executive Leadership Program at the University of San Diego.

Born in New Jersey and raised in New York, Ken received a master's degree from Colgate University and a bachelor's and PhD from Cornell University.

Ken can be found at www.kenblanchardbooks.com or via @kenblanchard on Twitter.

Claire Diaz-Ortiz is an author, speaker, and technology innovator who has been named one of the 100 Most Creative People in Business by *Fast Company*. Claire was an early employee at Twitter, where she spent five and a half years.

In Claire's time at Twitter, she was called everything from "The Woman Who Got the Pope on Twitter" (*Wired*) and "Twitter's Pontiff Recruitment Chief" (*The Washington Post*) to a "Force for Good" (*Forbes*) and "One of the Most Generous People in Social Media" (*Fast Company*).

Claire is the author of seven books, including *Twitter for Good: Change the World One Tweet at a Time, Design Your Day: Be More Productive, Set Better Goals, and Live Life on Purpose,* and *Hope Runs: An American Tourist, a Kenyan Boy, a Journey of Redemption.*

She is a frequent international speaker on social media, business, and innovation and has been invited to deliver keynotes and trainings throughout the world. She writes a popular business blog at ClaireDiazOrtiz.com and serves as a LinkedIn Influencer, one of a select group of several hundred global leaders chosen to provide original content on the LinkedIn platform.

Claire holds an MBA from Oxford University, where she was a Skoll Foundation Scholar for Social Entrepreneurship, and has a BA and an MA from Stanford University.

She is the cofounder of Hope Runs, a nonprofit organization operating in AIDS orphanages in Kenya.

She has appeared widely in major television and print news sources such as CNN, BBC, *Time, Newsweek,* the *New York Times, Good Morning America,* the *Today* show, *The Washington Post, Fortune, Forbes, Fast Company,* and many others.

Read more about her at www.ClaireDiazOrtiz.com or via @claire on Twitter.

SERVICES AVAILABLE

The Ken Blanchard Companies® is committed to helping leaders and organizations perform at a higher level. The concepts and beliefs presented in this book are just a few of the ways that Ken, his company, and Blanchard International—a global network of world-class consultants, trainers, and coaches—have helped organizations improve workplace productivity, employee satisfaction, and customer loyalty around the world.

If you would like additional information about how to apply these concepts and approaches in your organization, or if you would like information on other services, programs, and products offered by Blanchard International please contact us at:

The Ken Blanchard Companies
World Headquarters
125 State Place
Escondido, California 92029
United States
Phone: +1-760-489-5005
E-mail: International@kenblanchard.com
Website: www.kenblanchard.com

JOIN US ONLINE

Visit Ken's Website

Learn about Ken, read his blog, and browse his library at www.kenblanchardbooks.com.

Visit Blanchard on YouTube

Watch thought leaders from The Ken Blanchard Companies in action. Link and subscribe to Blanchard's channel and you'll receive updates as new videos are posted.

Join Ken Blanchard on Facebook

Be part of our inner circle and link to Ken Blanchard on Facebook. Meet other fans of Ken and his books. Access videos, photos, and get invited to special events.

Join Conversations with Ken Blanchard

Blanchard's blog, HowWeLead.org, was created to inspire positive change. It is a public service site devoted to leadership topics that connect us all. This site is nonpartisan and secular, and does not solicit or accept donations. It is a social network, where you will meet people who care deeply about responsible leadership. It's also a place where you can express your opinion.

Ken's Twitter Updates

Receive timely messages and thoughts from Ken. Find out the events he's attending and what's on his mind @ kenblanchard.

Claire's Twitter Updates

Keep up with Claire and discover all manner of innovative ideas @claire.

Visit Claire's Website

Learn about Claire and read her blog at www.claire diazortiz.com.